ANALYSIS OF PROCESSES OF ROLE CHANGE

S. N. Eisenstadt, D. Weintraub, N. Toren
THE HEBREW UNIVERSITY, JERUSALEM

ISRAEL UNIVERSITIES PRESS
Jerusalem, 1967

ISRAEL UNIVERSITIES PRESS
is a publishing division of the
Israel Program for Scientific Translations, Ltd.
P.O. Box 7145, Jerusalem, Israel

IUP Cat. No. 2625

Printed in Jerusalem by S. Monson
Binding: Wiener Bindery Ltd., Jerusalem

ANALYSIS OF PROCESSES OF ROLE CHANGE[1]
S. N. Eisenstadt, D. Weintraub and N. Toren

PART I

Introduction

The purpose of this paper is to formulate a framework for the analysis
of role structure, role behavior, role crystallization and processes of
role change on the basis of theoretical considerations which have come up
in the course of a series of researches.

The paper consists of four parts. In the first section some new
approaches to the analysis of role change are suggested. Several specific
studies of cases of role change are then analyzed in terms of the approaches
suggested in the first part. In the final sections some hypotheses about the
conditions and directions of processes of role change, derived from these
case studies, are put forward as a possible basis for further research.

I

The concept of "role" has been in the forefront of sociological thought
and analysis during the last two or three decades. Different studies have,
of course, developed different approaches to this concept, emphasizing
various specific aspects in it.[2]

Despite such differences, most of the definitions of "role" used in the
various researches have some common denominators. Thus, they define
"role" as a constellation of factors organizing an individual's behavior in
society in some "general", socially approved patterns and goals.

This "generalized" social behavior has been recognized as consisting of
several components. Most of the definitions of the concept of role have
emphasized some of the following components:

a. The "positional" or "situational" aspect — namely, the specification of
some position or situation in the social structure, the incumbents of which
are expected to perform a given role.

b. The "contents" of the role, usually defined as its goals or output.

c. The "exchange" aspect of the role, i.e., the specification of the
relations with other people or other roles involved in the performance of
the given role.

The system of exchange has been described in many different ways — the
best of which is probably in terms of: (a) the outputs or goals of the given

role; (b) the inputs, i.e., the various types of resources which are necessary for the processing of the given output, and the more indirect "rewards" (in terms of money, prestige or power) given to the incumbents of any given role; (c) the specific processes by which the inputs are transformed into the outputs, the most important aspects of which being the immediate, organizational setting in which this process takes place and the broader setting, particularly the suppliers of the necessary resources and rewards and the recipients of the outputs.

The central importance of the exchange and interaction relations in the definition of any role emphasizes the fact that no role stands alone—that within each role there exist one or several complements in other roles without which its generalized goals and outputs would be meaningless; thus, any role constitutes an element in one or several role-sets.[3]

(d) The normative aspect of role, i.e., the fact that the specification of generalized goals and patterns of structural interaction and exchange are sanctioned, although to different degrees, in terms of some of the norms and values represented by the holders of central positions in the society or its sectors and that various types of sanctions are employed in order to uphold these normative injunctions.

(e) It has also been emphasized that the goals and output of roles are related to, or derived from, some basic "needs" or exigencies of social systems, and that they fulfil some functions for the maintenance of society.

Generally, a combination of the normative and the "organizational" and "functional" aspects has been designated as the focus of the conditions of institutionalization of roles.

Perhaps the most important outcome of these considerations is that a role does not constitute a discrete habit or pattern of behavior, but a system in which different actors interact around the central focus of the output (or generalized goal) of the role according to rules of interaction, exchange and performance, upheld by sanctions and norms. Any such system is crystallized on several different levels, and although few systematic analyses of such levels exist in the literature, some common ground does exist, the most salient being the normative, the cognitive and the technical levels.

The normative level entails the definition of the components of a role in terms of the predominant norms and values and the legitimation and sanctioning of the patterns of rights and obligations assigned to a role.

The cognitive level refers to the same components as perceived by the actor—i.e., the incumbent or incumbents of the roles. On this level it is possible to distinguish between the knowledge and intellectual perception of the role by the incumbent (of actions, norms, resources, etc.) and the expected or aspired pattern of the role, namely, his "role-image" (this distinction is roughly equivalent to Kurt Lewin's "perceived and expected milieu"). In the present context the term "cognitive" is thus not used to denote a purely intellectual perception in the technical psychological meaning of the term, but rather the overall subjective orientation of the actor to his role. The two patterns which make up this orientation—the perceived and the expected—are not necessarily always identical, and the particular relationship between them is a focal point of interest for consideration in empirical research.

The technical level constitutes the actual pattern of behavior and activities of the incumbents of roles and of those with whom they interact in a systemic way in these capacities.

II

Thus, whatever the differences in the exact specification of the different components or aspects or role, most of the major works dealing with the concept of role have recognized, implicitly or explicitly, that "role" and "role-behavior" constitute a system in which these different components are organized in some way. Yet initial definitions of role, as well as the researches dealing with various problems of role-analysis, tended, at least implicitly, to use the concept as a relatively uniform one, i.e., treating the role as a system whose components always go together and vary in an uniform and homogeneous way.

Only lately have several approaches, recognizing the inadequacy of the accepted definition and specifying the possibility of some independent variation in the components of role, been developed.[4] These contain important indications, tending in the direction of the systematic analysis which has been attempted here.

The present attempt is based on three main propositions or assumptions: First, that not all human behavior is formed into patterns which are called social roles. In fact, the performance of a role is only one type of behavior in general, and of social behavior in particular.[5] (Thus, for instance, many types of customs, habits or even of technical tasks performed may not evince the systemic and normative character which is characteristic of the role-set or role-system). Second, it seems that any such given role or role-set does not necessarily constitute a given and fixed pattern within the institutional structure of any society. On the contrary, the very formation of any specific role should be seen as a complex process of the crystallization of various components into a system with properties of its own. Thus, although certain role-components necessarily tend to go together, they may also vary independently. Third, while these variations are, of course, not infinite, and are limited by the social system within which the role is set, each of them may often be subject to independent influences and may thus constitute an independent focus of change, affecting the role as a whole in different ways and to different degrees.

On the basis of these assumptions some of the problems of role analysis, in sociological theory and research, have been reformulated.

Firstly, the actual crystallization of a certain pattern of behavior and its normative definition into what may very generally be called a "role" should be investigated. That is to say, studies should be made of the social conditions or mechanisms which create—from the potential of various demands, institutional exigencies and personal needs, existing in any given society or its parts—the specific crystallizations of the different components of roles, or, to use a somewhat different nomenclature, of different types of roles. Different components of any role or of any sub-role might consequently be studied profitably on the basis of the different degrees of institutionalization of each of them separately and in combination, and/or as to whether all or only some of them become institutionalized to any given extent. The same should apply also to the crystallization and articulation of different role-sets, i.e., to the various roles which become connected, as it were, with any given role and "impinge" upon it.

Second, it cannot be taken for granted that once a role is "formulated", or crystallized, it is set and fixed. On the contrary, it is necessary to study and analyze role-crystallization as a continuous process, in the different stages of which different situations, social forces and mechanisms are emphasized.

Third, the definition of role as an ordered set of components indicates the importance of the relation between these components and forces "external" to the system of any given role and the ways in which the interaction between them may influence changes of a role. This can be viewed as a two-stage process: first, in the influence of a given external variable (or set of variables) on a specific component of the role; and second, in the changes of the relations between different components resulting from the initial change in one of them. These processes, however, cannot be assumed to be necessarily either automatic or simultaneous and the relations between them have to be investigated.

Fourth, the approach proposed here suggests the necessity for a reformulation of the problem of "role-conflict", so often dealt with in sociological literature.[6] The present approach indicates that conflict may arise not only because an individual has to perform different roles which may make contradictory demands on him, but also because of the differing and potentially conflicting constellations of the components within any given role or role-set. The different types of conflict, as well as the conditions under which they develop, were accordingly regarded as constituting a significant subject for investigation.

Fifth, the same considerations can be applied to yet another question, namely, the individual's performance of different roles. Most previous studies in this field have dealt with the individual's adaptation to a given role, and with his ability (or inability) to perform it. In fact, the picture presented or implied in the literature in this respect has often depicted the individual as progressing through some basic age and sex categories and some fundamental institutional roles — economic, occupational, political, and religious. This image generally implied that through this process the "normal" (non-deviant) individual tends to perform the same type of more or less fixed type-roles.[7] It seems that such a conception is over-simplified and that it might be worthwhile to assume that the individual's progress in different roles necessarily brings him into situations which are, or at least may be, organized in different ways, from the point of view of his ability to fulfil his own aspirations. The performance of roles by individuals should not, accordingly, be viewed as a somewhat static assumption (or non-assumption) of certain attributes, and as a realization of certain types of fixed expectations and norms set by society. It should rather be conceived of — and studied — as a far more differentiated process in which the individual's aspirations and perceptions interplay in a variety of situations, emphasizing in each of them different aspects of normatively regulated behavior (indeed, this "encounter" between individuals and the supposedly "given" roles often creates the possibility of role-innovation, i. e., change in the constellation of different components of a role and of different sub-roles).

Sixth, the approach suggested here may provide some insights into the way in which the crystallization of different roles may, in its turn, influence the development of the institutional structure of society. The process of creation and crystallization of different roles is taking place continuously in all societies — even the most "stable" ones. Although, in some cases, the basic definition of a role in a society is more or less constant over long periods of time, the relative emphasis on its different components will vary according to the different situations and forces which impinge on it. Thus, instead of taking the role-map of a given society as if it were completely fixed and given, we propose to consider it as being continuously shaped by various forces and mechanisms which should be systematically studied.

Finally, the problem of the variables or forces which influence the different constellations of the major components of roles has been raised. In this respect it was felt that these components must be defined and analyzed in a way which would enable their consideration as not always fully organized in roles but as possessing separate, autonomous "life" of their own. Thus, for instance, it was considered necessary to envisage the different types of resources available in a society — whether economic, prestige or others — as distinct from their actual crystallization in roles. It is true that in concrete situations such resources are released or manipulated by people performing specific roles. What was found important analytically, however, was not the fact that these resources are commanded by roles, but rather their special characteristics as such — e. g., their liquidity, the extent to which they are monopolized by certain groups, etc.

The broad assumptions about role behavior as well as the more specific reformulations of research problems in this area outlined above had, of course, to be tested in research through the analysis of concrete cases.

This we have attempted to do (as described in the introduction) in two stages. In the first stage we have reanalyzed materials from several researches of the Department of Sociology of the Hebrew University, attempting to see whether it is possible to apply to them the scheme of components of role delineated above and to test the assumption that these components may, at least to some extent, vary independently and be influenced in different ways by different sources of change.

In the second stage of this examination, in the last part of the paper, we have attempted, on the basis of the preceding analysis, to present some hypotheses about the relation between different sources of change and the conditions of change and crystallization of different role patterns.

PART II

Seven roles were selected for the analysis of role-change and crystallization, namely those of New Small-Holding Farmers, Members of Collective Settlements, Civil Servants in Bureaucratic Service Roles, Public-Bus Drivers, Professionals — teachers and doctors, and Cadet Pilots.

The material consisted of a reanalysis of various existing research projects of the Department of Sociology of the Eliezer Kaplan School of Economics and Social Sciences, the Hebrew University, Jerusalem.[8]

I

New Small-Holding Farmers

New small-holders' Cooperative settlements (Moshavim) served as one case-study for the analysis of processes of role-change.[9]

The Moshav type of village[10] was originally created in 1912, and by the establishment of the State of Israel there were 58 settlements of this type. The cooperative movement in agriculture was initially smaller than the collective (Kibbutz) one; however, with the creation of the State and the influx of large waves of immigrants, more than 250 Moshavim were established, and the situation has been reversed.

The reasons for this fundamental change were complex. For a variety of economic, security, political and ideological reasons rural colonization became a major vehicle of both development and absorption of immigrants, and a significant section of the new-comers was channelled to agriculture and under- or undeveloped areas.

Since most of the people concerned had no previous agricultural experience, completely independent individual and scattered farming was not considered practicable for their settlement. The settlement was thought to require rather a closely knit community structure and a comprehensive cooperative network, within which absorptive agencies might best work, making the transition to agriculture easier and more gradual. The Moshav pattern was chosen as the most suitable for this purpose. It was considered more flexible than the collective pattern, and as a movement was most willing to absorb new, non-selected settlers. Thus, while the new settler role was formally conceived of as simply a replication of a role carried into a new situation, in fact it was a new role based on an existing normative pattern.

Several different sources of change have impinged on this pattern.

The first such factor was found in the change of the basic composition of the manpower as regards the "personality" type of the incumbents of this role. This was manifest in the demographic composition of the new immigration, which contrasted sharply with that which had established and maintained the original Moshav. The new immigration was culturally and socially heterogeneous and non-selective, including groups with small disposition towards, or preparation for, agricultural work and a rural way of life. Consequently, the performance of the settler role now depended upon a reservoir of actors differing from the original settlers in their background in relation to motivation, education, family, age, social structure, and community organization.

Another factor of change, also external to the role-system proper and yet particularly relevant to the Moshav, was found to reside in the overall economic developments in the country. Especially significant in this respect was the growth of internal markets associated with population increase, and the switch-over to an export orientation rather than economic autarky.

Thirdly, in addition to these overall social and cultural transformations, the data show the significance of the impact on the role of changes in its immediate external, i.e., ecological, setting. Most of the new villages were established in regions less suitable to mixed farming than to industrial crops, thus reinforcing the export-orientation in creating new farm-types. Other villages, chiefly those in mountain areas, were placed in circumstances of land and water scarcity, making an equitable distribution of adequate plots impossible.

These ecological situations, characteristic of many of the new villages, were often reinforced by the scarcity of other resources, such as lack of sufficient capital, time, know-how and personnel for planning, organization and training. For while the resources at the disposal of the settlement programme were, in absolute terms, far greater than had been the case during the Yishuv,[11] they were now spread over a much wider area in the service of a more ambitious undertaking.

As a result of these external changes in the overall society and in the immediate setting of the settlers' role, combined with internal strain within the role-system, many stresses in the old, "ideal-type" normative definition of this role developed. These stresses were reinforced by a discrepancy in the initial definition of the role — namely the inconsistency between the norm of democratic government on the one hand, and the norm of efficient economic and municipal organization on the other.

All these processes caused far-reaching changes in various aspects of the role.

A significant impact was first observed in the sphere of the output of the role: 1) Generally speaking, the absolute agricultural output of the Moshav sector increased as a whole, due to sheer quantitative growth. 2) The decline of Arab agriculture and the larger share of the Moshav in relation to the kibbutz also raised the relative weight of this production within the agricultural sector, correspondingly elevating the position and power of the Moshav movement in this sector. 3) At the same time, the importance of the symbolic output of the role declined, due to general social, political and ideological trends (described below with respect to the kibbutz). The economic product thus became the major output of the role, which suffered accordingly an absolute decline in status in comparison with urban occupational roles in general, and industrial, governmental and professional ones in particular. This process was further intensified by other factors. The numerical increase of the new settlers, while not itself sufficient to offset the growing political and economic dominance of the city in society and in the labor movement, has lowered the "marginal utility," or relative importance of the Moshav, thus contributing to the decline in social status of each individual settler. This applies particularly to those new settlers — still a large majority — whose individual output falls short of the regular norm in quantity and quality and whose income and standard of living is consequently lower.

Equally significant changes have occurred in the performance of the role. Firstly, far-reaching changes have been made as regards the principles of independent (non-hired) labor and farming as the sole occupation of the settler. This was brought about primarily because of family structures unsuitable for Moshav farming; while at one extreme there were households with insufficient manpower, necessitating their recourse to hired labor, at the other there were large households with under-employment and sub-standard per-capita income, which were obliged to seek additional or alternative outside employment. This trend was reinforced, moreover, by the transition from mixed to industrial farming, dictated by economic and ecological considerations—industrial crops having a notoriously uneven work-curve which cannot be met by family labor during the peak season. The change in farm-type has, of course, further resulted in the specialization of output and of tasks, which in turn has brought diversity to the Moshav movement as a whole, affecting its identity of interests and uniformity of economy to some extent. A similar process of change has taken place in the organization of the role within the individual village. At one pole, there has thus been a weakening of solidarity, cooperation and mutual responsibility, with the role being performed in an individualistic, gesellschaft-like way, while at the other, traditional settlers have established familistic and paternalistic patterns of performance and supervision.

The cognitive level of the role has largely paralleled the developments on the technical levels. Most of the new settlers—not having any pioneering or socialist ideology—are in accord with the new economic-occupational emphasis of the role per se. At least in this respect, therefore, they seem subjectively better adjusted than the veterans to the new character of the role. However, this instrumental orientation makes them particularly sensitive to reverses and to other occupational opportunities, and their attitude towards the Moshav is largely ambivalent.

Finally, the resources available for the individual role have diminished relatively, affecting the output and performance of the role. For though the means at the disposal of the State are now absolutely greater than before, they have to serve larger sections of the population, while the means provided by the actors themselves—chiefly motivation and skill—fall far short of the requirements. This last role change is of course directly traceable to changes in the type of actor allocated to the role.

Most of these changes on the technical and the cognitive levels have been accepted, to some extent, on the normative level too, chiefly by the Land Settlement Department. This has been the case particularly with regard to Moshav society and organization, outside work, and limited hired labor. On the other hand, no legitimation has been given to poor agricultural performance and low production, considered incompatible both with national interests and scarce resources, as well as with the projected well-being and position of the settlers. Even partial acceptance has been gradual, and is as yet informal and ambivalent—especially within the ideologically oriented Movement.

III

Members of Collective Settlements (Kibbutzim)[12]

One of the major foci of the study of the Kibbutz was the investigation of processes of social change and differentiation as they developed within highly

8

homogeneous groups, based on spontaneous solidarity and intense identification with egalitarian values, and with an ideology which was originally opposed to any explicit, rigid and formal definition of tasks and roles. The Kibbutz ideology maintains that the social activity of its members should be broad and many-sided rather than narrow and specialized, that men should be treated and evaluated as total persons and not as holders of specific roles and that spontaneity should rule instead of formalization.[13]

With the passage of time, many changes have taken place in these communities due to a variety of factors, each of which separately — and all of them combined — have given rise to several changes in the role of the member of the Kibbutz.

It is possible to distinguish between two such types of sources of change; internal ones — especially processes of maturation within the Kibbutzim, and various external processes. Two demographic processes have been of crucial importance with regard to the first source of change. The first was numerical growth, in the course of which the initial nucleus often grew from a few dozen members to several hundred. This growth was naturally closely related to economic development and to the growing division of labor. Second was the process of maturation and aging of individual members; this process resulted in the crucial structural change of the establishment of families and the rearing of children in the Kibbutz, and also in various changes in the personalities of individual incumbents of the role — among others, in their physical fitness and levels of aspirations.

Beyond the general demographic changes, the continuous existence of the collectives as communities spanning several generations has entailed the routinization, formalization and differentiation of roles, and the development of various sub-systems, such as the family or working groups. The original homogeneity was greatly weakened and altered by the growing division of labor, the articulation of the authority structure, the crystalli- zation of various solidary sub-groups and the establishment of families.[14] Concomitantly, distinct elites emerged within the originally "classless" setting — such as production managers, technical experts and "professional" political leaders — which in turn strengthened the trend towards the redefinition of the role-image and role-behavior.

The second focus of change was located outside the Kibbutz and was related to the impingement of external, societal forces on the Kibbutz. The most important source of change was the relative standing of the Kibbutz in the broader Israeli society after the establishment of the State of Israel.

During the pre-State period (Yishuv), the Kibbutzim, composed of veteran pioneers, possessed most of the criteria of high status: public activity, education, length of residence in the country and participation in some kind of collective establishment. As a consequence, in the period of the Yishuv, the Kibbutz member enjoyed an elite position,

With the establishment of the State, new values and elites have emerged, being embodied chiefly in the professional, governmental and entrepreneurial spheres. The new elites have become increasingly important reference groups and targets of mobility aspiration. This has influenced the standing of the Kibbutz and the Kibbutz member in a number of ways. On the one hand, the values symbolized by the Kibbutz were affected, some of them — such as equality and asceticism — losing in general importance and salience, while the collectives lost their monopoly over others — notably pioneering and national service. On the other hand, the concrete power of the Kibbutz in society diminished; it was now increasingly dependent upon the State for the provision of many resources, and it lost much of its bargaining power vis-à-vis other organizations.

This loss in power and status undermined individual identification with the Kibbutz in some cases and caused a search for avenues of mobility outside the Kibbutz; it generally, however, served to emphasize new criteria of status, based on education, specialization, and diversification into industry, thus reinforcing the internal economic processes described above. It has also, in many ways, put the ideologically more devoted members of the Kibbutz on the defensive.

All these developments have affected the role of the Kibbutz member in a variety of ways. The first general effect of these processes was obviously that of differentiation between the various specific roles of the settler. Secondly, as a result of the impact of these forces of change, discrepancies within the role-system itself were created.

These developments will be analyzed within two such sub-roles of Kibbutz members — the occupational and the family ones.

The original ideology of the Kibbutz required the egalitarian allocation of occupational roles and especially of managerial and leadership positions. At the beginning, this kind of allocation was duly adhered to by means of the continuous rotation of members among the various jobs and tasks. But in the course of time considerations of efficiency and specialization have over-ruled the principle of job-rotation.

These processes of change impinged on the occupational role itself. On the technical level, a process of differentiation and specialization in some of the components of the role has taken place; the output has become more specific and defined, the processing of these outputs became more expert and the allocation of the tasks more differentiated, and the supply of resources more rational and specialized.

In contrast, however, to the differentiated supply of resources to the various actors on the basis of their specific tasks, the distribution of rewards to the actor has remained largely egalitarian. The discrepancy between differentiated means and responsibilities and uniform rewards has become a potential source of strain within the role-system.

More complex changes may be noted also on the cognitive level of the occupational role. The Kibbutz member has, of course, become sensitive to the processes of specialization and differentiation which his occupational role has undergone; he recognizes their necessity and inevitability and to a large extent even welcomes them as enabling greater achievements by the community and a higher realization of individual potential. However, since the Kibbutz member's image of his society is still very strongly anchored in the original values of egalitarianism and collectivism, the attitude towards specialization and differentiation is both ambivalent and perceived to conflict to some extent with the basic social image of the Kibbutz.

As a result of these processes a basic distinction has developed on the normative level between the legitimation of changes relating to resources and performance of the role, and those relating to the status of the role-incumbent. While the differentiation and specialization of resources and performance have been accepted and incorporated into the official ideology as representing orientations of achievement, rationality and efficiency necessary for the development of the Kibbutz, differentiation in rewards and status is ideologically rejected. At the same time, there is a difference in this respect as regards various types of occupational roles. At the two poles, namely the managerial-elite role on the one hand, and the low status service roles on the other, care is taken to prevent the crystallization and formalization of status positions. Rotation in jobs of this type is maintained as a mechanism symbolizing basic equality.

In the middle range roles, by contrast, such as branch managers, longer tenure of jobs and regular differentiation of rewards have been accepted.

In the family sphere changes also developed, mainly towards the differentiation, expansion and crystallization of the role's resources and output. The family unit and role were initially influenced by demographic changes in the Kibbutz society, as the setting up of families, the rearing of children and the process of aging. These processes impinged on the cognitive level of the role, changing the attitude to, and perception of, the family role. These changes, in turn, constituted pressure towards changes on the technical level of role-organization and behavior.

One of the main postulates of the original Kibbutz ideology was the complete equality and interchangeability of role-allocation between the sexes. In practice, a fairly clear-cut sex-role differentiation has emerged, in both the occupational sphere and that of intra-family tasks, in spite of the repudiation of such a distinction in the original ideology. Similarly, certain functions, such as the socialization and education of children, which were formerly performed by the collective, were partially taken over by the family unit.

With the addition of tasks and outputs, the resources at the disposal of the family also grew. The family developed to a certain degree into a consumption unit, owning some kitchen utensils, food and clothing, and also a small budget for personal expenses.

On the cognitive level, the family role has also gained in importance. Women have been generally found to be more family-oriented than men, but even in the role-image of men, conflicts have sometimes arisen between the orientation to the family and the broader orientation to the collective.

On the normative level, change has been much smaller, and thus far there has been little ideological legitimation of the "familization" of such basic functions as socialization and placement. These functions are still expected to be in the hands of the collective as a whole.

Less extreme has been the normative resistance to the strengthening of family integration and solidarity as a social unit, which have come to be regarded as beneficial to the community. In this respect mechanisms of secondary institutionalization have developed; although the children still continue to live and receive education in communal children's homes, the time they now spend with their parents is much greater and each family home now contains a children's corner and toys. In the same way, there has been legitimation of eating in the family room; and while communal meals are still the universal pattern, it is now possible for families to eat together in the communal dining-hall, and have a family afternoon snack or entertain visitors at home.

This analysis of the occupational and family roles of the Kibbutz members shows that within the context of the general process of differentiation of spheres and roles in the Kibbutz society different roles have undergone different types and degrees of change.

Occupational and family roles have changed on the actual-behavioral (technical) level far more than on the normative level. By contrast, the occupational sex-role differentiation has been ideologically legitimated to a greater extent than the egalitarian sex-role differentiation in the family. Consequently, the discrepancy between the different levels of the role is smaller in occupational roles and greater in family roles.

This general tendency has assumed different patterns and degrees in different Kibbutzim, depending on their internal structure. The extent of the normative legitimation of the changes has been found to be related to the degree of institutionalization and formalization of values and norms in each Kibbutz. In general, the smallest legitimation of these changes has developed in those Kibbutzim characterized by unqualified loyalty to a set of general norms, intense collective identification and comradeship, non-formality of norms regulating social life and homogeneity regarding age, marital status and country of origin.

Nevertheless, all the various collectives have had to develop to a greater or smaller degree several informal mechanisms of secondary institutionalization, which minimize, "explain away," or isolate this gap. Among these mechanisms mention should be made chiefly of the following: rationalization, that is the representation of change in terms of the existing ideology; strengthening of ritual and symbols representing basic values, and their attachment to novel forms of behavior, thus making it possible on the one hand to segregate the new situations from the basic ideology, while on the other hand developing some frameworks in which the older values are symbolically maintained. These mechanisms developed precisely because there is an intensive and "traditional" attachment to values, combined with the lack of formalization mentioned above. As a result, it is possible to maintain the original ideology side by side with new behavior patterns and criteria of day-to-day evaluation. In other words, the gap between ideology and reality, or between the normative and the actual levels, is often itself institutionalized rather than bridged — especially with the help of mechanisms which tend to blur symbolically the specialization and differentiation which has developed in reality. For example, the role differentiation between the sexes is to some extent "adjusted" to the original principle of equality by means of symbolic participation of men in feminine roles (such as temporary service of men in the Collective kitchen and dining room), and, on the other hand, by the symbolic and temporary participation of women in masculine occupations (such as work in agricultural branches).

III

Bureaucratic Service Roles

The study on Bureaucracy and Immigration in Israel was concerned with the problem of the confrontation of officials in various service-agencies (such as social workers, public health nurses, policemen, etc.), with new immigrants from non-Western countries, who had had little previous contact with formal organizations.[15] The study analyzed the way in which the formalized and differentiated role of the bureaucrat, which was beginning to crystallize at this period, has in turn been influenced by the introduction of a new type of clientele—namely new immigrants coming from "traditional" settings.

The change in the type of clientele aroused several spheres of tension between the bureaucrat and his client, reinforcing the inherently different definitions of these two interacting roles—the formal, institutionalized role of the bureaucrat and the less formalized, more individualized role of the client. This divergence was accentuated as a result of the influx of immigrants from non-bureaucratic countries, who became dependent on bureaucratic organizations for the fulfilment of many of their needs.

The clients' perception of their own role as well as that of the bureaucrat was, to a very large extent, governed by traditional attitudes and criteria, i.e., mostly by particularistic, ascriptive, diffuse and personal norms. Moreover, the situation of strain and insecurity in which many immigrants found themselves, due to the crisis of migration and the transition from a traditional to a modern society, engendered a feeling of helplessness and almost total dependence on the absorbing society. The bureaucrats were seen as the representatives of this society, and were often expected to provide total help and the solutions to diverse problems.

This discrepancy between the role-expectations of the interacting role incumbents was, of course, manifest not only on the cognitive but also on the technical-behavioral level. For example, the client refused to pay for the services he received (even though the required sum was usually only "symbolic"); he refused to stand in line and await his turn; he sometimes used threats or even physical force to get what he wanted.

These changes in the role setting, and the pressures generated by them, caused changes within the system of the role of the bureaucrat.[16] The most immediate outcome of this situation was changes on the technical level as regards output, performance and resources.

The output of the role became more diversified and diffuse—the various bureaucrats were now fulfilling functions not originally within their terms of reference. Specific service-agencies, such as sick-funds and labor-exchanges, often had to deal with general problems of absorption, e.g., family relations and budgeting, education of children and vocational training. Thus the "proper" function of the bureaucratic role often took a secondary position and had to be performed in a rigid and mechanistic way.

Similarly, the situation now required new types of resources, which were not always at the disposal of the average bureaucrat—such as empathy and familiarity with the heterogeneous cultural backgrounds of the various immigrant groups. This problem was further aggravated by the insufficient economic and administrative resources at the disposal of the bureaucratic agencies.

On the cognitive level of the bureaucrat's role, various mechanisms of adjustment to the new situation evolved. Four different role-conceptions, particularly with regard to the output and performance, were found to have crystallized. These were:

(a) The "ritual" pattern, over-emphasizing the administrative orientation and minimizing the client-oriented role-dimensions;

(b) The "rebellious" pattern, completely client-oriented and opposing the organizational restrictions;

(c) The "professional" pattern, attempting to strengthen the role incumbent's status by way of professional knowledge and orientation, and thus minimizing the feeling of pressure;

(d) The "educational" pattern, trying to lessen client-organization friction through emphasizing the education of the clients to their role.

It was found that the "ritual" pattern tends to develop in those structures or among those people where the formal definition of the role is adhered to cognitively.

The "rebellious" pattern seems to develop where changes have taken place on the cognitive and behavioral levels alike. In these cases the bureaucrat not only alters the performance of his role so that it is more suitable to the clients' demands and needs, but is also convinced that these changes should be formally legitimized by the bureaucratic institution.

The "educational" and "professional" patterns tended to develop in those cases where the bureaucrats changed their cognitive orientation in response to the new pressure exerted by the client, while at the same time accepting the importance of professional and/or bureaucratic standards and commitments.

However, these processes of change did not always occur simultaneously on the technical and the cognitive levels. In most cases, the actual-technical level changed first, thus creating discrepancies between the behavior of the bureaucrat and his role-perception. This internal discrepancy has sometimes — but only sometimes — been bridged over by parallel changes on the cognitive level. On the other hand, in some cases changes in the bureaucrat's role perception have not been accompanied by changes in the actual processing of the role.

Similarly, the changes on both the technical and cognitive levels were not always matched by parallel ones on the normative level. The normative level of the role, as expressed by the formal definition of the bureaucratic norms of the organization, has been found to change too. Thus, for instance, several bureaucratic agencies have recognized the importance of, and officially adopted, more continuous and diffuse relations between the bureaucrat and his clients. In this way, sick-fund community clinics for new immigrants were established, with relatively little rotation of staff and close, personal contact with the population in the clinic and the home. The importance of non-bureaucratic resources was also recognized by various organizations, and bureaucrats were required to receive psychological and sociological training in addition to their professional training proper.

But on the whole official legitimation of some of the non-bureaucratic expectations of the clients did not develop, chiefly as regards demands based on particularistic criteria; this was largely due to great sensitivity of the central bureaucratic agencies to open deviation from formal rules. Thus, perhaps the most general characteristics of the process of crystalli-zation of bureaucratic roles, the minimal general — even if differentiated — crystallization of norms, and the actual process of such crystallization took place mostly through informal and partial innovations by groups of role-holders.

In several of the situations studied, the officials created "defense techniques," that is, unofficial, or semi-official, structural changes which

diminished the pressure on the line-man. Mechanisms of this kind were:
1) the "collective defense," namely the formation of an unofficial, decision-making peer group intended to give backing to clients and supervisors alike; and 2) "buffer technique," i.e., the unofficial delegation of one of the peers to receive "appeals" from the clients and transmit communications to the bureaucracy. These informal mechanisms were sometimes partially institutionalized, thus producing a "model" which became the major focus for formalized structural change.

The various semi-structural changes did not, however, develop in any orderly homogeneous way. The extent to which any of these types of structural arrangements crystallized was dependent on a great variety of factors — such as the personal background of the officials, and the ecological location of the office — many of which were randomly distributed. On the whole, however, the process has, it seems, been made somewhat easier by the fact that the bureaucratic role itself has not yet been fully crystallized and formalized, irrespective of the confrontation with the new immigrant clientele. The changes described have not been entirely in the nature of a "deviation" from a fully institutionalized "ideal" bureaucratic role, but have rather constituted developments or stages in a role undergoing a process of crystallization and institutionalization.

IV

The Role of the Public-Bus Driver

Within the general research on bureaucratic services a special section was devoted to the role of the public-bus driver. This research focused mainly on the analysis of changes in the driver's role due to the confrontation of the driver with a new type of clientele, namely new immigrants from non-Western countries.[17]

The driver's role was especially interesting because of two particular factors:

a) The fact that almost every new immigrant has to interact with this bureaucratic-service role in the initial stages of the absorption process into the new society;

b) The technical character of the driver's role and its relatively rigid definition, further accentuating the incompatibility of the driver's role and the client's expectations from it.

As in the other roles described, several external factors combined here to produce the new developments:

a) The general changes in the value-system of the society, which affected the public-driver's role by greatly weakening its symbolic significance on the one hand, and by placing it on relatively lower echelons of the emerging new hierarchy of professions, on the other;

b) The rapid general economic and technological development and the growth of the population, which brought about a marked growth of the various bureaucratic-service organizations including the public transportation cooperatives.

These two changes have also affected the personality of the incumbents of the role, in the sense that the rapid expansion of the organization was accompanied by a rational emphasis on technical skills rather than on personal qualities, or on loyalty to a socialistic-cooperative ideology.

These "external" sources of change, together with the influx of new immigrant clientele, affected the various components and levels of the driver's role differentially, thus creating internal discrepancies in the role-system.

On the technical level, no considerable change in the central output, processing and resources of the role occurred. But, as was demonstrated in the analysis of other bureaucratic-service roles, various tasks were added at the margins of the main formal goals and tasks of the role. The "non-bureaucratic" clients expected the driver to advise them on diverse problems (such as the work situation or political situation), to give information (as regards various public agencies and their functions) and to help them generally in their orientation to the new environment.

As a result, the performance of the role tended to change—becoming less formal and specific.

The changes on the cognitive level were parallel in some respects to those which had occurred on the technical level. This was primarily the case with the driver's conception of the main function of the role and of its status. For, while some respondents continued to perceive their role in terms of some symbolic significance (such as pioneering, collectivism, socialism and manual labor), and demanded high social prestige in consequence, the majority stressed the technical content of their work, emphasizing instrumental rewards instead (such as salary and working hours and conditions). New orientations towards clients and role-performance developed, which were—as in the case of the service bureaucracies—differentiated into several types:

a) The "personal" or diffuse orientation, based on, and embodying, face to face relations and obligations.

b) The "service" orientation—the conception of the driver's role as providing a public service, emphasizing such aspects as precision, caution, readiness to give information and politeness. This pattern is nearest to the "ideal-type" of the bureaucratic role.

c) The "educational" pattern—emphasizing the driver's task of teaching, and thus changing the "non-bureaucratic" behaviour of the new clients.

d) The "technical" pattern—the conception of the driver's role as a purely technical-mechanical role, emphasizing driving and mechanical skills.

Different factors influenced the crystallization of these orientations.

The "personal" orientation was found to be chiefly related to a factor inherent in the immediate situation of the role, namely the degree of continuity of the driver-passenger interaction. Drivers who worked for long-term periods (from 2-8 years) with the same clientele had more personal-diffuse relationships with the passengers than those whose interaction with their clientele was only short or sporadic.

The development of "service" orientation, by contrast, was associated with the composition of the drivers' clientele. It was found, paradoxically enough, that the drivers working with new immigrants tended to develop a "service" orientation, whereas those working with veterans did not.

The interpretation of this seemingly paradoxical finding is that in Israeli society the ideology of "public service" has not yet crystallized. One of the main reasons for this is the tradition of the egalitarian ideology of the Yishuv period, which was originally opposed to the concept of the service of one individual by another.

The driver, whose role suffered a decline of status, is particularly sensitive in this respect. This status-anxiety is emphasized in his interaction with "veteran" passengers, whereas in his relationship with new immigrants he is freed from this anxiety or "inferiority-complex."

The "educational" concept of the role, on the other hand, has been found to be related to the driver's status within the cooperative; for example, those drivers who commanded a higher status in the organization (various managerial and control roles) had an "educational" role conception. This accords with the findings from other studies that people in elite positions usually have an "educational" orientation, and see the transmission of values and norms of behavior to others as one of their tasks.

In the case of the bus company, as in other bureaucratic-service organizations, the various changes in the role-performance and conception have been only partially legitimized by the organization. The "policy makers" of the cooperative have, to some extent, recognized the importance of the more continuous, and hence more personal and diffuse, patterns of interaction between the driver and his new immigrant clients. The driver's character and temperament, his knowledge of the clients' language, etc., were also taken into consideration. Under certain circumstances even deviant behavior by the driver was sanctioned and recognized as necessary. Most of these legitimations, however, were usually ad hoc and only semi-institutionalized. This is in part due to the fact that the public-driver's role is essentially a very technical and rigid one, and that these qualities limit the contents, direction and amount of change that can be institutionalized.

V

Professional Roles

Another study relevant for analysis was that of the Social Structure of the Professions in Israel.[18]

The purpose of this study was to analyze the relationship of the changes within Israeli society in the process of transition from the Yishuv to the State of Israel, and the development of professional roles within it.

The professions studied intensively were medicine, teaching and law, in public and private employment; here we shall deal with the first two only.

One of the focal points of the original research was the change in the status and status-image of the various professional groups in relation to the broader social structure.

During the pre-State period the status enjoyed by teachers, doctors, lawyers and other professionals, was not quite as high as it had been in their countries of origin or as it is in other modern societies. This was due to the dominant ideology of that period which was, as we have seen,

opposed to most private enterprise and individualistic occupational roles.
This ideology recognized the role of the intellectual in general, and the
professional in particular, as important and useful in realizing such
collective goals as cultural revival and the creation of a physically strong
nation. But the specific structure of the modern professional role —which
incorporates the economic aspect of payment according to generally fixed
standards, the human-relations aspect of mutual trust, and the cultural
aspect of scientific training —was only partially sanctioned by the dominant
ideology. All this was found to cause ambiguities in the definitions of the
different professional roles, accounting for some of the differences in their
relative positions in the hierarchy of Yishuv society.

From among these various roles, the teacher's role became identified as
a pioneering, collectivity-oriented role, although without the same prestige
as agricultural work in collective frameworks. But, because of the
affiliation of the teacher's role to the collective goals and ideology, the
more professional and technical aspects of the role were under-emphasized.
The functions of the teacher's role were defined as largely integrative and
expressive and called, therefore, for such prerequisites as identification
with the ultimate values and loyalty to the collective. Professional training
and qualifications were not considered indispensable for the performance of
the role.

By comparison with the teacher's, the doctor's role was less bound up
with the dominant ideology. It was difficult to assimilate the doctor's role
completely to the general structure and values of society. Although most
of the medical services were conducted within public frameworks, and
although socialized medicine was the formal ideology of the profession, the
acceptance by doctors of all the implications of collective and pioneering
values was always rather ambivalent. By the same token, the official
ideological attitude to some of the professional aspects of the role was also
ambivalent, as manifested by the partial admission of the doctor's more
autonomous standing and scientific and professional orientations.

With the establishment of the State and the transformation of the Yishuv
from a "revolutionary" movement into a fully-fledged social system, the
relative status of the professional roles changed. First, there was the
general change in values, goals and status criteria, described above.
Second, the need for professional roles and services increased so rapidly
and to such an extent that the demand has consistently been in excess of
supply, thus considerably improving the bargaining position of the
professionals.

These ideological and structural changes were reflected in changes on
the various levels and components of the different professional roles —albeit
in different, sometimes contradictory, ways in the two professions.

The importance of teaching was emphasized, since it was perceived to
be one of the principal media of socialization and absorption of new
immigrants from different cultural backgrounds. This called for new
resources and higher professional standards. On the other hand, however,
the increase of needs caused by mass immigration and by the introduction
of compulsory education laws, brought about a rapid and unselective
mobilization of man-power for teaching.

Thus, on the technical level, discrepancies developed between the
resources at the disposal of the untrained teacher and the qualifications

required for the appropriate performance of the role. This resulted in the lowering of the quality of the teacher's output, according to the new professional standards.

The "unprofessional" role pattern of the teacher's role was emphasized also because — stemming from the role-image and perception of the "veteran" role-incumbents — the cognitive level of the teacher's role was strongly anchored in the dominant value orientations of the Yishuv society. This orientation included, at least implicitly, low evaluation of the formal training of teachers and the more technical and instrumental aspects of the role. Adherence to the "traditional" pattern of the role caused the development of discrepancies between the cognitive level of the role — particularly that of the "old-timers" — and between the new needs, requirements and changing values of the society.

The lowering of qualifications and standards for entrance to, and performance of, the role combined with inappropriate value orientations affected the hierarchic position of the teacher's role by lowering his status. This was reflected in the relation between teachers' economic rewards and those of other professsions and occupations.

However, these developments were not characteristic of all teachers. The changes were accompanied by a further development, namely the emergence of a distinct group of high-school teachers with academic training and qualifications. These teachers were relatively young and were not burdened by loyalty to the collective ideology of the past. They placed greater emphasis on the professional aspects of the teacher's role, such as formal specific training, the need to effect changes in the curriculum in accordance with new conditions, and the development of more precise standards of achievement. The divergence from the "traditional" orientation and performance of the role was also manifested by the development of an independent union.

The pattern of change in the doctor's role differed in several crucial aspects from that of the teacher. This was primarily due to the general position of the doctors and the different internal structure of their role — as compared with that of the teachers.

Generally speaking, the doctor's role was also influenced by the process of absorption of new immigrants. The mass immigration to Israel was characterized by disproportionately large numbers of sick and old, thus causing a great numerical increase in the doctor's clientele. This factor was particularly significant in the light of the establishment of Welfare State principles and policies, emphasizing the responsibility of the State for public health. Nevertheless, the great demand for doctors did not result in the lowering of qualifications for the entrance and practice of the role. The doctor's role was established as a professional role — with professional and scientific criteria of performance — already in the pre-State period, and the structural changes which accompanied mass-immigration and the transition to Statehood did not impinge, despite some pressures, upon the quality of the role's output. Moreover, the changes in the value systems of society — namely the decline of collectivistic and egalitarian value orientations — were now more consistent with the professional orientation of the doctor's role. Indeed, the most outstanding effect of the expanding scope and specialization of medical science, and of governmental care for the sick lay in the increasing number of doctors working in large bureaucratic organizations, such as hospitals, clinics and sick-funds, as against those in private practice. This change and differentiation of the settings in which doctors worked initiated further changes on the cognitive level. It was found that doctors who had a stable clientele (that is, chiefly, the private practice setting) tended to have a strong service-orientation and role-image; doctors employed by large-scale bureaucratic organizations (chiefly sick-fund clinics) developed organizational loyalty, while doctors in research hospitals stressed the scientific aspect of the role, attaching primary importance to the esteem and viewpoint of professional colleagues rather than of patients.

The elevation of the doctor's status, as well as the processes of differentiation and specialization that this role underwent, were to a great extent legitimized by the "formal ideology." Nevertheless, the normative level of the role did not change to the same degree as the cognitive level. To some extent the conflict between the collectivistic-orientation of the Yishuv period and the norms governing professional roles still remained. This was expressed in the Government's attitude to the professionals' demands for "appropriate" financial rewards. In this respect, the expectations of the role-incumbents were far ahead of the crystallization of new normative criteria.

With their increased bargaining power as a result of the structural developments and value changes described above, the doctors have succeeded more than teachers in achieving the recognition of their professional status and the furthering of their economic positions.

VI

Cadet Pilot [19]

As a case-study in role change, the cadet pilot differs from the other roles discussed in several important respects. First, changes in role-structure can be traced entirely to one dominant source of change, namely the various technical innovations connected with the development of aeronautical science, as they affect the main technical "complement" of the role — the plane.

The increasing complexity of the plane machinery and of the training course necessitated the expansion of the economic, professional and organizational resources in the flying school, at the same time emphasizing the actor and his role-set.

The study has shown the growing difficulty for the cadet of making more demanding split-second decisions, and tolerating the instability and uncertainty deriving from frequent changes in the main complement of the role, as well as from the awareness that norms and performance rapidly become obsolete. However, in sharp contrast to the bureaucrat under pressure and the new farmer, the cadet pilot is not allowed to change the pattern of performance and the set standard of excellence in respect to the output. In fact, the role is shown to be extremely inflexible, permitting no discrepancy between the normative and the actual levels of behavior. In other words — unlike the roles mentioned above — here the impact of external factors of change has been "contained" and restricted by the role-system.

Particularly striking is the "resistance" of the immediate setting of the role, i.e., the cadet's role-set, which has remained essentially the same with respect to hierarchy, size of group membership, and patterns of interaction. In fact, irrespective of the technical innovations, a similar peer group constitutes the main social setting of the actor during the earlier stages of the course, and the instructor-trainee dyad during the later ones. Nor is there any distinct change in the mobilization and social composition of the role-set, irrespective of ongoing developments in the size and character of the population in general.

Because of this very exacting and at the same time extremely rigid definition of the role, the cognitive level of the role—namely the actor's role-conception—has assumed a particularly strategic importance.

The place occupied by this role in the cadet's status image was found to be of crucial importance. Two dimensions of this status image were considered most relevant here:

a) the extent of the "realism" of the image, or—more precisely—of its occupational components;

b) the extent of the flexibility of this image.[20]

Without entering into details, it has been found that these different status images, or subjective evaluations of the pilot-role, tended to form a descending scale of motivation adequate for the performance of this role.

It was found that an image which is both realistic and flexible permits the cadet to meet the necessary exigencies and the deferment of rewards inherent in a training period, while preventing him from being excessively attached to, or emotionally dependent upon, success as a trainee. The other extreme, on the contrary, is characterized by a lack of perspective, by a short-sighted role conception, and by an inability to defer rewards. This ritual and rigid combination in fact renders difficult any adjustment to "new situations" which emerge in the course of role-activity, and increases the dependence upon immediate gratification. Furthermore, the fear of losing the expected rewards, as well as of facing a vacuum in case of failure, create a situation of ceaseless anxiety adversely affecting role performance.

Within the framework of the basic predisposition, attitude to the course and to flying as a career is sometimes modified during the training. The most important mechanism in strengthening or weakening motivation is the nature of the role-activity—namely, whether the learning process is smooth or difficult. In order to increase the cadet's involvement, some secondary changes in the structure of the learning situation have been introduced to assure better instructor-trainee compatibility in the dyad, such as the allocation of "fatherly" and authoritative instructors to suit the trainees' dispositions and expectations whenever possible. Similarly, communication with the cadets has been increased and regularized, care being taken to make information available on the criteria for the selection of candidates, the evaluation of results, and the organization of the course. The understanding thus gained by the cadets into the working of the course has diminished feelings of tension and of discrimination, and raised their trust in the "distributive justice" of the organization. All in all, however, the significance of the course as a mechanism is marginal, and affects primarily border or ambivalent predispositional types. Better selection or allocation to the role on the basis of predispositions is thus the main mechanism of reaction to change in institutionalization. In fact, the main change introduced in the course under the impact of the growing technical requirements has been to structure it in such a way as to assure optimal selection as early as possible.

PART III

In the preceding section we have analyzed briefly several cases of role change. In the following section we shall attempt to analyze this material systematically, arriving at some tentative conclusions about the general characteristics of processes of role change, and the conditions of change under which different types of crystallization of roles take place.

Any initial impact of sources of change on a given role-system which has some enduring effects entails a change in the relations between the various components as well as in the boundaries of the role as a system. This may be in the existing rates of exchange between the inputs and outputs of a role, between the resources needed for the implementation of a role and the rewards accruing to its incumbents, in the levels of performance of a given role or in the relative importance of various role-partners or role-sets.

The strains created by such changes in a role-system necessarily call for some readjustments. Such changes do not in themselves assure the development of new norms which would define and rearrange the relations between the components of a role in some articulate way which would be applicable to different situations, and which would be upheld and sanctioned, at least to some extent, by some groups or individuals within the society.

Thus, in such situations of change each role or role-system faces the problem of how much innovation—in the sense of the establishment of some such norms—can develop within it, and in what direction and on what levels will such developments take place.

With regard to almost all the roles studied here, relatively similar broad sources of change could be discerned—the most important external influences being the transformation of the major values orientations prevalent in the broader society, changes in organization, mobilization and allocation of resources and rewards within it, and changes in the personalities of the incumbents. At the same time, different configurations of these sources of change operated with regard to the different roles studied here; moreover, each of these sources had a specific, differential impact on different components and levels of any given role.

Furthermore, whatever the importance of the initial impact of these external sources on any given role, they in themselves did not determine the further crystallization of the roles. Here some additional factors, and especially some aspects of (a) the internal structure of the role-system prior to its change; (b) the status of the role in society; (c) the social characteristic of the role-holders; and (d) the nature of the immediate role-setting, were found to be of great importance.

Thus, recrystallization of roles is composed of two interrelated but analytically separate dimensions, or steps:

(a) the strain which is created in the role-system, following the initial change in some of its components;

(b) the "chain reaction" of further change which this strain triggers off
—that is to say, the adjustment to the strain on different role-levels.

These two steps or dimensions have to be distinguished from one another,
in so far as the initial impact may be "absorbed" by different roles in
different directions, creating different patterns of recrystallization. In the
following analysis we shall attempt first to see whether some regularity
exists in the differential primary impact of various sources of change on
different components or roles, and second, to analyze the condition of the
recrystallization of the role following this initial impact.

I

In the case of the small-holding farmers the change in the personalities
of the role-incumbents was manifest in the nature of the resources supplied
by them and their expectations, affecting both role performance and output
on the technical level, and role-conception and evaluation on the cognitive
level.

Changes in the broader society in the allocation of resources to the role
affected primarily the technical level, limiting the supply of inputs to the
role and increasing outputs, while diminishing the rewards of each actor,
(particularly in the material sphere). These changes in rewards given to
the incumbents of the role were reinforced by changes in the broader societal
system of stratification which diminished some of the symbolic rewards
given to this role.

These changes were related to, but not identical with, the general value
orientations predominant in the society, which tended to impinge initially on
the ideological basis of the normative definition of the role. But this
impingement had a much more delayed impact; the preexisting normative
definition, as formulated by the first settlers and the officials of the settling
agencies, tended to persist for a relatively long time.

The differential impingement of different sources of change thus created
a discrepancy or strain between the normative level, which was more
resistant to innovation, and the two other levels of role-crystallization, and
to some extent between the cognitive and the technical levels.

The pressures for innovation encountered multiple resistance on the
normative level because on this level the original definition of the role,
represented by the older settlers who became the representatives of the
settlement authority in the new villages, was (a) diffuse, deeply anchored
in ideology and directly committed to values; (b) very strongly
institutionalized; (c) rigid in allowing limited interchangeability in output
and performance; and (d) highly interdependent as regards the various
concrete technical tasks (such as the agricultural worker, the marketer of
products or household owner).

By contrast, several factors related to the new incumbents of the role
combined to produce a drive towards innovation. This was so because these
incumbents were (a) mobilized in a non-selective way, and in a situation
where the supply of openings exceeded demand; (b) they had not been
socialized into the pioneering value system; and (c) they were organized to
exert or resist pressure through participation in political parties, etc.

Moreover, these incumbents had: (a) a partial monopoly on outputs which were vital for the performance of the role; (b) independent command over most of the required resources; and (c) considerable control of sanctions.

Similarly, several aspects of the role-setting were, as we have seen, conducive to innovation. These were: (a) the small scale of the setting; (b) the fact that it was intimate, homogeneous and non-bureaucratic; and (c) its distance from political and administrative centers, thus allowing for some degree of experiment without impinging on the more central symbols and frameworks of the society or of the whole Moshav movement.

The pattern of recrystallization of the role of the new small holding farmer was thus characterized by a considerable initial role-strain and by the pull of two opposite forces in response to this strain. On the one hand there were the change-oriented incumbents of the roles who were in a position to determine the actual performance of the role and to secure the supply of resources; in this respect the gap between the cognitive and the technical levels was closed to a considerable extent. On the other hand the ideological inflexibility of the role-system emphasizes normative resistance to change. As a result of this, the actual change was legitimated and institutionalized only in a partial and a differential way. No legitimation was given, and role-strain continued with regard to changes in the main functions of the role — which remained chiefly productive and occupational. Symbolically meaningful but secondary outside employments were frowned upon but tolerated while technical innovations, e. g., deviations from planned farm-structure, could, when successful, be incorporated in the formal scheme.

II

Some interesting parallels — as well as differences — can be found with regard to the role of the Kibbutz member. Here, changes in organization and in the allocation of resources from the broader social structure have also initially affected the technical level, acting upon it in a partially contradictory way; while the supply of inputs to the role increased in absolute terms, as well as in respect to individual units, it decreased in comparison with other sectors of the society. Similarly, the relative "status" place of the Kibbutz member declined with regard to specific outputs of the role and rewards, whose relative importance was diminished by the rise of competing roles with similar functions. In a marked contrast to the role of the small-holding farmer, however, there was no marked change in the personality of the incumbents (or if there was, it lay primarily in processes of maturation and aging); and the cognitive level was not directly influenced at this stage, but was rather acted on indirectly through the changes on the technical level.

Here, even more than in the case of the role of the small-holding farmer, there was resistance to change on the normative level, in spite of changes in general societal values directly relevant to the role-definition. The pioneering, egalitarian and collectivistic definition of the role persisted in spite of the value transformation in the broader society — even becoming to some extent "rigidified" in reaction to it.

Thus, the initial changes began with a "technical innovation," creating a gap between this level and the cognitive and normative ones. The process of recrystallization of the role of the Kibbutz member evinced markedly different combinations of innovation and resistance to change. The structure of the role-system was, still more than in the preceding role: (a) very highly value-oriented and ideologically committed; (b) rigid, and (c) interdependent—a combination conducive to high resistance to change. Moreover, unlike the situation in the Moshav, (d) mobilization to the Kibbutz remained highly selective and admittance remained restricted to properly socialized candidates, role-holders being identified with the normative pattern and committed to its maintenance rather than its change.

The range of innovation open to the role-incumbents in order to adjust to the strain created by changes on the technical level was thus inherently limited, on the whole, to the existing broad framework of the role-pattern itself. However, innovation did exist within the Kibbutz, as a result of several facilitating factors, since the role-setting was (a) highly solidary; (b) non-bureaucratic; and (c) intense and homogeneous; it was also characterized by (d) considerable autonomy in decision making. An ability to mobilize considerable resources in money, skilled manpower, organization, dedication and creativity existed within the settlement and throughout the Movement. In consequence, the strain within the role triggered off extensive experimentation calculated to minimize stress and produce viable solutions to the basic incongruence through technical innovation and its secondary institutionalization, and through development of special new symbolic ritual occasions through which such secondary institutionalization became possible.

There was, moreover, a great difference between the Kibbutz and the Moshav with regard to the spread of the elite.

In the Moshav there was a significant difference in background and orientation between the settlers and the Movement elite and Settlement agency hierarchy; the problem has thus been primarily one of external normative acceptance. Among the Kibbutz members there was no sharp distinction in composition or ideology between the individual village and the Movement or the Settling agency. In other words, the actor, or each group of actors, was not responsible to a supervisory body.

III

The role of the bureaucratic civil servant was first influenced by changes in the broader society in the allocation of functions and resources to different roles—especially as a result of the formation of a State-wide civil service—by the increase in the number of clients, and by the change in their type. All these affected firstly the technical level of the role, especially methods of performance, enlarging the outputs and increasing the rewards of office—chiefly prestige and, to a lesser extent, its emoluments. These last (especially the prestige aspects) were reinforced by the general trends of development in the status system by the increase of the status of State service.

The changes in the personnel of the bureaucratic structure impinged, initially, on the cognitive level where changes in conceptions — although less extreme than in the case of the small-holding farmer — took place as regards (1) role-performance and (2) rewards. Changes in the value-orientation of the broader society—particularly in criteria of status—were also of direct relevance to the normative level, tending to redefine the role in line with the growing professionalization and emphasis on technical criteria, although the impact was slow and intermittent.

Within this general context of public service, the role of the bus-driver was relatively little influenced by the changes in the availability of resources—Jewish bus cooperatives having had a monopoly on motor transport within the Jewish community during the Yishuv. Here the main change occurred in the output of the role, which formerly had involved para-military and pioneering elements connected with the maintenance of communications to scattered settlements under conditions of disturbance, and which now became "usual" bus service.

The changing nature of the clientele due to mass immigration, on the other hand, affected the technical level of the role, particularly:

(1) the scope of activity and outputs, which increased enormously;

(2) the conditions of criteria of performance of the role; performance became both more bureaucratically organized and impersonal, as well as subject to the cross-pressure of clients from non-bureaucratic backgrounds.

As the output of the role became almost entirely technical rather than partly symbolic and pioneering, the status of the driver decreased correspondingly; at the same time, a tendency towards increased emphasis on semiprofessional and technical criteria developed. This tendency was reinforced by a considerable influx of new drivers, a new type of role-incumbent, with stronger technical and vocational cognitive orientations.

In these roles too (i.e., those of the bureaucrat and the public drivers), the initial change created a discrepancy between the technical and the other two levels. However, the strains thus created, and the patterns of recrystallization, were quite different from those of the roles of the Kibbutz member and the small-holding farmer.

Despite the assumed rigidity or inflexibility of bureaucratic roles, the initial change in this case was not accompanied by strong normative resistance, nor was the role-system in itself particularly susceptible to strain. This was due to: (a) little previous institutionalization and rigidity, and (b) few independent symbolic connotations. The crux of recrystallization lay in the gap between the cognitive and the technical levels of the different partners of the role—namely, between the bureaucratic orientations of the role-incumbents, and the non-bureaucratic background of the immigrant clientele. This incongruence brought about changes—mainly in the role-conception and performance of the bureaucrat in different, often contradictory, situations without the emergence of any new, consistent, overall type, or types, of role-definition or crystallization.

This stemmed from the fact that although the provision of services—and of absorptive services in particular—was a vital function and could have given the incumbents considerable power potential, this potential was limited because: (a) for a considerable time most of the services were split among competing agencies—governmental, municipal, public and voluntary; (b) the role-holders had no real control over resources, such as the allocation of personnel or of physical facilities in the offices; and (c) they worked with a clientele which could not be easily or quickly transformed or influenced, and which had to be attended to. Thus the role-incumbents had little real sanction; moreover, the role-setting within which they worked was not very conducive to the development and maintenance of a common unified and new role-definition, or set of definitions. The incumbents involved with the new clientele were a limited group of line-personnel, not always enjoying the solidarity of peers, let alone the support of the hierarchy, while at the same time being under pressure from the center to keep things going quickly and not to contravene – at least formally or openly –the formal directives of the center.

The role of the public-bus driver also shows a cognitive adjustment in response to strain created by changes on the technical level. This case shows how different types of cognitive adjustment — or different role-images —developed in response to the same strain, due mainly to the variability of the role-setting, particularly as regards the background and position in the hierarchy of the role-incumbents, and the duration, regularity and intimacy of their contact with clients.

IV

The role of the teacher was first affected by the same broad structural factor as was observed in the case of the bureaucrat — large-scale immigration — inducing changes in the size and character of the school population. On the technical level these affected: (1) inputs to the roles, (2) role-performance. The influx of new personnel, representing a new type of role-incumbent partly recruited from among the new immigrants themselves and partly from the younger generation just out of school (or the army), brought about changes in cognitive orientations to the role — particularly in the direction of emphasizing occupational (and mainly monetary) rewards and to some extent professional ones. These orientations existed together with the persisting conceptions and expectations characterizing the older, more ideologically motivated teachers. The changes in the broader status systems were in turn potentially inimical to the status of the role of the teacher, based as it was on largely non-professional, ideological criteria.

On the normative level, represented mostly by some of the officials in the Ministry of Education and by some more pedagogically-oriented teachers, the basic, slow and uphill process of educational experimentation and institution building began. It developed as a response to new, objective requirements, such as the evolution and testing of methods and media and experimentation with new types of schools and class arrangements, thus tending towards increasing professionalization. These changes were not, however, paralleled by similar ones on the teachers' cognitive level or by their response to these new normative definitions.

This was due, primarily, to some aspects of the structure of the role-system of the teachers: (a) the role had never been rigidly defined, and could therefore formally incorporate change, but (b) it was highly value-anchored and diffuse — oriented to the total personality of the client and his home-setting.

This, together with the objective difficulties in the performance of the role and its diminished prestige, led to a development of a more materialistic-instrumental rather than a more professional role-image. This was largely due to the following factors:

The character of the role-holders, primarily the fact that: (a) they found it difficult to compete on favourable terms in a free teaching market defined in a rigid professional way; (b) the Teachers' Federation was one of the largest and best-organized Trade Unions, located centrally in the Federation of Labour and with main lines of connection to the ruling political party; and (c) although the role-holders had not formal control over material and organizational resources or over norms and sanctions, the importance of the function itself and the role's complete monopoly over it increased their bargaining power considerably.

These tendencies also influenced the relative importance of different settings of the role, emphasizing the power of the bureaucratic centers — of the Ministry and particularly the Trade Union Organization — and minimizing the innovative potentialities of the smaller, informal and less center-oriented pedagogical settings of the single class or school.

It was only, or primarily, within some of the groups of secondary school teachers that the process of role-crystallization developed towards professionalization, with some emphasis on pedagogical innovation, although here, too, the "material" aspects of professionalization were accentuated.

This was due not only to the fact that within these groups there was a longer tradition of professionalization, but also because the different basis of selection to the profession made their bargaining position within the market much more favorable, and therefore they were not inclined to accept the directives of the General Trade Union.

Thus, in the course of the recrystallization of the role of the teacher new strains were created, minimizing the possibility of mobilization of resources and of improving levels of performance.

V

The doctor's role was also influenced initially by the growth and diversification of the service and by the impetus due to immigration, which changed the size and nature of the clientele and thus affected: (1) the scope of activity (general output), (2) the adequacy of resources and, (3) the conditions of performance of the role. The influx of medically — and otherwise — "deprived" population within a context of a welfare policy and a strong public sector tended to concentrate most of the new medical openings within organized frameworks. The increasing objective requirements of medical science and specialization tended also to work in a similar direction, emphasizing the importance of large hospitals and clinics. These trends, operating primarily on the technical level, were partially paralleled by independent tendencies on the cognitive level — the emphasis on research and specialization becoming a salient feature of the medical training system and thus an integral part of the orientations of the new generation of doctors.

Changes in the broader societal system of stratification tended to reinforce professionalization.

The professional's claim to special status was now recognized basically, and the orientations of the role-holders, which had previously been somewhat marginal within the context of the prevalent collectivistic and egalitarian ideology, began to accord with it.

However, several areas of strain developed, and the recognition of professional status served to emphasize the gap between what was subjectively due to the doctor in the material sphere and what the needs and pressures of other groups made it possible to give. Thus, professional Trade Union activity became a significant reaction of the role-holders to technical and normative changes.

In addition, a certain amount of incongruence between the technical and cognitive levels developed as regards performance. This was due first to the fact that the doctors and teachers, like the bureaucrat, were confronted with a new-immigrant clientele, greatly pressing towards some "deprofessionalization," and second to the pressure from public bodies to "bureaucratize" the doctor's role at the expense of specialization and professionalization.

While, on the whole, the change was towards professionalization, attempts were consistently made to withstand these pressures, as was evidenced by several types of reactions. On the one hand there was an acceleration of the tendency to leave public clinics in general, and those in immigrant regions in particular; many outlying or "under-privileged" communities have either been consistently under-staffed or else became the initial stepping stones in the career of new-immigrant doctors. On the other hand the doctors who preferred, or were compelled, to remain in these clinics worked constantly to adapt the situation to the professional image and by utilizing the status of the role and the power of the profession they caused the introduction of organizational innovations calculated to improve conditions in the practice and in patient-doctor communications (e. g., by limiting the patient quota, by the establishment of the family doctor in the clinic, by the establishment of regional clinics, etc.).

This general tendency in the crystallization of the doctor's role was the result of several factors. The structure of the role-system was:
(a) diffuse, (b) highly institutionalized and (c) very rigid, and therefore initially allowed for only limited and temporary "deprofessionalization," with performance both ethnically and technically circumscribed.

This setting, with its relative homogeneities, small extent of bureaucratization and relatively high degree of autonomy was, however, not unlike the setting of the Kibbutz role — conducive to innovation within the professional framework, (i. e., in the direction of specialization or the development of new organizational types).

The doctors were able to maintain resistance to deprofessionalization because of several additional, broader factors. Among these the most important were: The character of the role-holders and their status which:
(a) was highly selective, (b) was organized in a large and powerful organization, (c) possessed an absolute monopoly over its output and enjoyed general esteem because of the vital importance of this output, and (d) had control over norms and sanctions (at least as regards membership and performance). However, here, as in the case of the teachers, the serious systemic strains between levels still continue.

VI

The cadet pilot was subject initially—and almost solely—to the impingement of changes of a scientific and technological character. These manifested themselves in the increasing demands and complexity of the pilot's tools of trade, directly requiring: (1) an increase in resources and, (2) the elevation of the level of performance.

Thus, the source of strain within this role lay in the growing difficulty of performing it, due to the increasing complexity of its technical inputs. The role was thus, for much of the time, in a state of "technical innovation" —with requirements likely to be one jump ahead of the normative methods of performance and the resources of the role-holders. Of crucial importance within this context was the fact that—unlike the other roles discussed—perfection of performance (or the closest possible approximation to it) constituted an absolute goal because the inflexibility of the role-system was total. The role was: (a) fully institutionalized, and (b) almost completely rigid—in the sense of admitting no deviation. Indeed, the avowed purpose of the normative specifications was to secure this end, leaving the role-holder no leeway.

Thus, except for matters demonstrably related to the tools and the efficiency of the trade, the margin for experimentation with techniques and ways of realization was, in this case, institutionally limited. No strong predispositions to innovation could be found in the configuration of such other factors as the nature of the role-setting which was: (a) large-scale, hierarchical, bureaucratic and very isolated, with little peer-support and cohesion in the small units, and (b) in the main line of communication and social control; or in the character of the role-holders which was: (a) highly selective, (b) identified with the role and competing for entry, and (c) almost completely lacking any access to direct or indirect power. Moreover, the status of the role was completely dependent on: (a) outside resources, and (b) outside norms and sanctions, and these factors (together with the role-holders' identification with the norms) centralized the power potential outside that of the actual role-holders.

Since all these combined to produce a strain towards conformity, the gap which existed between requirements and incumbents' resources (and which was the outcome of factors below the conscious level and outside their volition) had to be bridged in one possible direction, while ensuring that the utilization of methods was maintained as much as possible within the institutionalized pattern.

PART IV

It is now possible—though clearly in a tentative way—to go beyond the general insights concerning the differential impingement of various sources of change on role-elements; and to spell out the relationship between the two in more specific terms. It seems indeed that there is an association between sources of change and the role-levels initially affected by them and that at each level the change in components is, by the same token, an ordered one.

1. The technical level is susceptible primarily to changes in technology and in the volume and allocation or resources in society. The stratificational position of the role is of major importance in this respect. Within this level, inputs constitute the component likely to change first, being most directly involved in the nature and distribution of resources. This source of change is also relevant to role-performance, while output and rewards are not immediately involved and are thus likely to change as an indirect outcome rather than a primary one.

2. The normative level is bound up in the closest way with changes in general values; its "reaction time" to this transformation is, however, relatively slow. With this reservation, changes in the normative definition of inputs and outputs are likely to occur first, the specifications of the function of the role in particular being most intimately associated with general values and goals. The definition of rewards or of the status of the actors is less saliently or directly involved, being in direct relation mainly with changes in stratificational criteria. Norms of performance, being significant on the technical rather than the symbolic level, are the least exposed to the source of change on this level.

3. The cognitive level is sensitive mainly to changes in the personality of the role-holders — that is, in the allocation of a different type of incumbent to the role. Since a difference in personality involves a change of orientation — of role-conception and expectations — it implies primarily a changed attitude to the rewards or status of the role. Orientations dealing with performance are directly under the impact of change mainly as regards their conceptual aspects, or in so far as this performance is taken to affect personal convenience or other considerations. This primarily instrumental significance is also the major sense in which resources have subjective meaning for the holder, removing him farthest from their initial impact.

However, the cognitive level is also susceptible to changes in values and to internal role-developments (as seen in the role of the doctor). At the same time, these are mainly secondary effects, and usually represent later role-processes.

Accordingly, the broader changes which impinge on the different levels of the role generally do it through different types of allocative and integrative mechanisms. Thus, the technical level is the most directly susceptible to changes in the supply and demand relations of inputs and outputs of roles through markets. This applies particularly to markets of services, commodities, money and, to some extent, manpower, and the various types of centralized allocation of such resources through central, bureaucratic institutions.[21]

The changes in personality which impinge on the cognitive level of a role do it most through changes in manpower, in levels of expectations and demands by the development of new skills, i.e., mostly through "massive" secular changes in population composition and the development of aspirations in more selected groups within these populations.

The normative level of roles is more directly susceptible to the various mechanisms of the "centers," namely the political, cultural and prestige centers.

However, as mentioned above, the initial impact of various sources of change on the different levels of a role does not in itself tell us about the concrete process of its recrystallization.

31

Here, as has been shown in the preceding analysis, several additional factors such as: (a) the nature of the role-system, (b) the social character of the role holders, especially in relation to the different resources needed for the performance of the role, and (c) the structure of the role setting, tend to "mediate," as it were, between the initial factors and the later process of recrystallization. Generally speaking, therefore, the basic problem which arises in this connection is one of the degree to which the impact of these initial changes does indeed induce the crystallization of new types or configurations of roles, and, more specifically, the exact direction and scope of such recrystallization.

Within this general framework, two questions seem to be most significant: first, to what extent within the given role-system does a predisposition rather than a resistance to innovation develop? Second, to what extent is this innovation capable of being institutionalized in some continuous and stable way?

The preceding analysis indicates that resistance to change, within any given role-system, is higher when any given role-system is (a) diffuse; (b) deeply anchored in ideology; (c) fully institutionalized; (d) rigid and allowing only limited interchangeability in output and performance; and (d) interdependent in its various concrete tasks.

These characteristics seem, however, to foster resistance to change in rather different directions. A high level of diffuseness may greatly impede the acceptance of new goals or functions, but—within the scope of the originally defined role—may permit, or even promote (as we have seen in the Kibbutz) a great range of technical innovations—i.e., the creation of new technical norms of performance or inclusion of new tasks.

Close interdependence between different aspects of the role seems, on the other hand, to inhibit the development of "smaller," narrower mechanisms of adjustment on the technical level, while being less inhibitive of the acceptance of new general goals.

However, the presence of configurations that are "positive" in this respect does not in itself assure the development of long-range innovation or the redefinition of the role-system as such.

The possibility that some such innovative tendencies will develop is to no small degree dependent on the nature of the organizational and institutional setting within which the potential innovators are located.

Apparently the more the setting is (a) highly solidary, (b) relatively small-scale and homogeneous (non-bureaucratic), (c) autonomous in decisions, and (d) distant, but not dissociated, from the organizational or political centers, the more will it be conducive to the generation and acceptance of innovations.

At the same time, variations as regards the different levels of a role may be observed. Technical and cognitive innovation—i.e., changes in subjective perception of the role and in its actual performance are perhaps less dependent on the cohesiveness of the setting and more on distance from the centers and autonomy in access to resources, while it is mainly with regard to normative innovation that all those factors seem to be important.

Needless to say, these two types of conditions—those which facilitate acceptance of change and those which are conducive to the institutionalization of new norms and patterns—do not always go together within the same role-set. To some extent there may be some contradiction between these conditions; thus those factors which facilitate the creation of conditions for innovation — especially the cohesiveness and solidarity of the setting — may also be conducive to high resistance to change.

Moreover, even when no such explicit contradiction exists within any given role-set, the existence of innovative potential does not yet assure the possibility of the stable institutionalization of changes in the role-setting.

In fact, some additional prerequisites seem to be necessary.

A very important condition of the institutionalization of change — indeed a necessary one — seems to be that the different partners of a role or role-set should not be bound within the same organizational setting, and that the control over different resources should be distributed among them.

When no single partner has full monopoly over any single one of the resources which are crucial for the functioning of a given level of a role, and partners may have differential control over these resources, the possibility of institutionalizing innovations becomes greater.

This has certain implications for the analysis of the major mechanisms through which the different sources of change impinge on different roles. Thus, the greater the extent to which the different partners participating in a changing role or role-set have access to different mechanisms through which these resources are allocated, the greater the chances that new relations between the components of the role will become crystallized and institutionalized, other conditions being equal.

However, here an important caveat should be included. Not every type of "spread" of access to resources is necessarily conducive to the institutionalization of innovation. In those cases where the different partners participating in a role or role-set have a more or less complete monopoly over one or more of the resources, the chances for successful institutionalization of change are relatively small.

This is accentuated if there is a combination of a monopolistic spread of control with a high degree of discrepancy between those who control and create the demand for outputs on the technical level and those who control the cognitive processes and thus role-performance.

Perhaps the "worst" situation from the point of view of relatively stable and continuous recrystallization of role systems is when the relative strength of innovators of, and resisters to, change is more or less balanced In such cases there is a strong possibility of the disorganization of any given role into component activities (such as processing or performance which is divorced from marketing or exchange) with only minimal continuous, systematic interrelations between them.

In these cases, as has been shown to occur to some extent in the bureaucrat's and the teacher's role, a "breakdown" situation may develop, expressed in diminishing efficiency of performance or in the development of a communicative gap between the cognitive and the normative levels. In extreme situations, though not in any of the cases presented here, this disorganization may engender the decomposition of any given role into its constituent elements and its disappearance as a distinct system.

If, however, the partners, whether old or new, participating in a role have differential access to all or some types of resources (especially those resources which tend to impinge on all role-levels) then the chances of readjustment to innovation and the crystallization of a new more stable relationship between levels and components will be greater.

In the material presented here this has been most clear in the cases of the small holding farmer and of the doctor. In both these cases those in formal control over norms and "normative" sanctions had only partial control over other resources, while others had a large measure of control over various technical and material resources as well as access to various types or sources of prestige. Consequently, a situation could develop in which the coexistence of role-partners was achieved, engendering significant innovations in almost all components.

The development of coexistence does not necessarily assure a change in the basic definition of the role, that is, reflects an almost "total" redefinition of goals and other components, nor does it represent complete legitimation of new activities and directions by those who, within the given social setting, have formal control over norms and sanctions. Indeed, when those role-partners who are so placed control other resources also (as in the case of the Kibbutz, for example), they may easily limit the range or the possibility of the institutionalization of change to technical or secondary aspects. The most extreme type of the cases presented here was that of the role of the cadet pilot, where those who controlled inputs and received outputs on the technical level also had almost total control over norms, prestige and sanctions (while in the Kibbutz it was the role-holders who had this monopoly, in the flying school it was the supervising partners).

In fact, a normative redefinition of the output or the goal of a role is highly dependent upon the existence of some consensus between the holders of material and other resources, and those who, within the given structure, claim to represent central social norms and sanctions appropriate to the setting. The present studies show that this situation is endemic in the Moshav and to a lesser degree in the Medical profession. To a still smaller extent, the bureaucratic service roles also evidenced this trait — primarily due to the "openness" of those in control of norms; here, however, the semi-monopolistic hold of the central agencies over the technical and material resources, together with the non-existence of role-settings conducive to sustained innovation, worked against such crystallization.

The differential control by various partners of a given role-set over the resources necessary for its organization and functioning also affects the concrete directions of the crystallization of new roles as regards their contents, the interrelations between the partners and their organizational settings.

First of all, it influences considerably the concrete bargaining positions and rates of exchange which develop between the different partners within any given role-set.[22]

Second, it influences the precise organizational frameworks of the exchange, e.g., bureaucratic as against non-bureaucratic, as is indicated by the roles of the driver and the civil servant. The elaboration of this point is, however, beyond the scope of this paper.

To sum up, it seems that the preceding analysis does bring out some of the relations between processes of role-crystallization and processes of institutionalization. It indicates that basically the former are a part of the latter, while, at the same time, the institutions themselves are not fixed entities, and should be seen rather as processes of institutionalization. The continuous development of different types of norms, organizations and frameworks regulates the flow of exchange of various resources and commodities in a society or parts of it.[23] The considerable variety of components and role-levels involved in crystallization indicates that this process of institutionalization comprises various aspects and takes place on several distinct levels. Role-crystallization at its "fullest" (i.e., when occurring more or less concurrently on all levels) is probably the "apex" of this process. But the fact that "complete" crystallization of this kind is relatively rare reemphasizes the variegated nature of institutionalization.

This point is also very closely related to and sheds some light on the problem of the definition of consensus within different roles—a problem which has baffled many researchers.[24] Thus, while it is quite obvious that consensus is an important aspect of the legitimation of any given role or role-set, and as Gross, Mason and McEachern have shown, different degrees of consensus may exist, the most important lesson seems to be that it is probably irrelevant to speak of such consensus in terms of acceptance by all members of a society. Indeed, a general consensus appears to be pertinent only as regards some universal roles—such as familial and basic political roles (although even here its actual achievement is doubtful). As regards more differentiated and specialized roles, however, the crucial problem is not the general "spread" of consensus in the overall society, but rather the extent to which some consensus develops among actual or potential role-partners. Thus, individuals or groups who participate—to a greater or lesser extent, directly or indirectly—in the broader setting of the role, and those who might have some access to positions of legitimation and prestige relevant to this setting and thus probably also to the more central spheres of society, constitute the critical role-partners in the development of consensus.[25]

Notes

1. The analysis presented in the following pages is based on a research project on Role Behavior and Social Structure, carried out in the Department of Sociology of the Hebrew University under the direction of the senior author; the Air Force Office of Scientific Research, Office of Aerospace Research, United States Air Force, sponsored the research. Dr. R. Bar-Yosef, Dr. O. Shild and Mr. Y. Peres participated in the early stages of the project, particularly in the formulation of the problems set out in part one of the paper.

2. The most general theoretical definitions of role can be found in: Linton (1936), Parsons (1951).

   The most important theoretical studies and definitions of role can be found in: Merton (1957), Sarbin (1954), Nadel (1957), Southall (1959), Bates (1956).

   For a very recent development of some aspects of role-theory see Goodenough (1955).

   For some studies which have described and analyzed various patterns of human behavior in terms of the different roles which the individual occupies, see: Chartier (1950), David (1955), Hall (1955), Komarovsky (1946), Reisman (1949), Wardewell (1952).

3. On the role set see: Merton, op. cit.

4. Several studies indicating new approaches to role analysis may be mentioned here: Ben-David (1958), Dahrendorf (1958), Gross, Mason, McEachern (1958), Levinson (1959), Turner (1962).

5. Despite this rather obvious point there have been to date few works which have fully recognized its implications. Thibaut's and Kelly's (1959) definition of role contains one important indication.

6. C.f. Goode (1960).

7. See, for instance, Southall, op. cit.

   For a new approach similar to our own see, for instance, Hodgson, Levinson and Dale (1965).

8. This reanalysis has been carried out on the sole responsibility of the present authors.

9. This re-analysis is based on a study of New Immigrants' Small-Holders' Cooperative Settlements carried out by Dr. Weintraub et. al. See chiefly: Weintraub (1964), Weintraub and Lissak (1961), (1964).

10. The Moshav is primarily a cooperative society with limited liability established to promote farming as the sole occupation and source of living of those organized in it. The nuclear family, of which there are on the average 100 in a village, is the basic social and economic unit, as regards production, consumption and socialization; but the various households are closely bound together by mutual solidarity and aid, as

well as by common agricultural, marketing, supply, credit and commercial services. The village economy is almost always based on the mixed-farm type, believed to promote national and individual autarchy in the supply of food, and to bind the farmer by diffuse ties to his yard. Each Moshav maintains an equitable division of the means of production (chiefly with respect to the size and quality of plots, water, resources and public capitalization). There is also little differentiation between the various developed villages themselves, the settlements being constructed so as to require a generally similar capital and manpower outlay, and to provide a like level of income.

In addition to its specific features, the Moshav also embodies the general colonizatory values characterizing the Kibbutz, namely national ownership of land, productivization, manual labour, pioneering, and simplicity of life.

Besides being an agricultural cooperative and upholding a definite way of life, the Moshav also constitutes a unit of local government, with the function of providing various municipal services. The authority over both the cooperative and the municipal spheres lies in the hands of the general assembly of adult members, which decides upon matters of principle and lays down general policy. The implementation of this policy is entrusted to the village council, assisted by various committees and an administrative staff. The mandate of the council derives from the power vested in it by the Assembly in free, universal and secret elections. The two constitute, in fact, the executive and the legislative body respectively, and their separation, together with the principle of democratic representation and responsibility, is an integral part of the Moshav value system.

11. Yishuv — the Jewish Community during the British Mandate.
12. The main features of Collective Settlement (Kvutzot or Kibbutzim) are: common ownership of property, except for a few personal belongings, and communal organization of production and consumption. Members' needs are provided for by communal institutions on an egalitarian basis. All income goes into the common treasury; each member gets only a very small annual allowance for personal expenses. The community is run as a single economic unit and as a single household. Husband and wife have independent jobs. Main meals are taken in the communal dining-hall. In most Collectives, children live apart from their parents and siblings, and from their birth on they sleep, eat and study in special children's houses. Each age group leads its own life and has its autonomous arrangements.

Collectives may vary in size from 40 to 50 members in a newly founded settlement to more than 1000 in larger and older ones. The founders of each Collective settle as a group. Additional groups and individuals join them afterwards. These groups are generally organized in youth movements and undergo training in longer established Collectives.

Each settlement is governed by a general assembly (which is convened as a rule once a week), by a council, and by various committees. Each Collective is affiliated to one of the Federations of Collectives.

13. This re-analysis is based on an extensive study on Collective Settlements in Israel, carried out under the direction of Prof. Talmon-Garber (1956), (1959).

14. This analysis is taken from "Differentiation in Collective Settlements" by Talmon-Garber (1955).
15. The study on Bureaucracy and Immigration in Israel was directed by Prof. S. N. Eisenstadt and Prof. E. Katz. See Katz and Eisenstadt (1960), and see also Bar-Yosef and Shild (1962).
16. It should be mentioned that the client's role has also undergone various changes — in the course of time the client learns and accepts some of the bureaucratic norms and accordingly changes his attitude. But in this context we are mainly concerned with the Bureaucrat's role, and the client's role is analyzed only as one of its complements.
17. This re-analysis is based on M. A. Thesis of N. Toren on "Processes of Change in the Role of the Bus Driver in Israel," conducted under the supervision of Prof. S. N. Eisenstadt.
18. The study on "The Professions in Israel" was carried out by Prof. Ben-David (1955).
19. This analysis is based on our ongoing project on "Problems of Air-crew Training in the Israeli Air Force," under the direction of Dr. M. Lissak and N. Slutski.
20. Operationally, we have defined the dimension of "realism" as the extent of congruence existing between the plans of the cadet within the air-force and outside it. Attention was paid to "subjective" reality, namely to the consistency of the cadet's own planning, rather than to the objective possibility of its being carried out. The dimension of "flexibility" was defined as the degree of openness to other occupational choices apart from that of fighter pilot.
21. See Eisenstadt (1959).
22. For a fuller exposition of these aspects of role institutionalization see Eisenstadt (forthcoming).
23. For a more detailed analysis see Eisenstadt (ibid) (1965).
24. See Gross, Mason and McEachern (op. cit.).
25. See Shils (1962).

REFERENCES

BATES, R. L. (1956). Position, Role and Status — A Reformulation of
Concepts. **Social Forces,** Vol. 34, No. 4.

BAR-YOSEF, R. and SHILD, O. (1962). Role Deviation in Bureaucratic
Occupations, **International Congress of Sociology,** Washington (mimeo).

BEN-DAVID, J. (1955). Professions and Social Structure in Israel.
Scripta Hierosolymitica, Vol. III, Hebrew University.

BEN-DAVID, J. (1958). The Professional Role of the Physician in
Bureaucratized Medicine: A Study in Role Conflict. **Human Relations,**
Vol. XI, No. 2, 255-275.

CHARTIER, B. (1950). The Social Role of the Literary Elite. **Social
Forces,** XXIX, 179-186.

DAHRENDORF, R. (1958). Homo Sociologus. **Kölner Zeitschrift für
Soziologie und Sozialpsychologie,** 10, 178-208.

DAVIS, F. J. (1955). Conception of Official Leaders' Roles in the Air
Force. **Social Forces,** XXXII, 253-258.

EISENSTADT, S. N. (1959). Bureaucracy, Bureaucratization and
Debureaucratization, reprinted from **Administrative Science Quarterly,**
4, 3.

EISENSTADT, S. N. (1965). The Study of Processes of Institutionalization,
Institutional Change and Comparative, **Essays on Comparative,
Institutions.** 3-69. Wiley, New York.

EISENSTADT, S. N. (forthcoming). Social Institutions, International
Encyclopedia of the Social Sciences.

GOODE, W. J. (1960). A Theory of Role Strain. **American Sociological
Review.** 25, 4.

GOODENOUGH, Ward H. (1955). Status and Role: Toward a General Model
of the Cultural Organization of Social Relationship, in the Relevance
of Models for Social Anthropology. A. S. A. Monographs, London
Tavistock Publications, 1-25.

GROSS, N. C., MASON, W. S., McEACHERN, A. W. (1958). Explorations in
Analysis — Studies of the School Superintendency Role.

HALL, R. L. (1955). Social Influence on the Aircraft Commander's Role.
American Sociological Review, 20, 292-299.

HODGSON, Richard C., LEVINSON, Daniel J. and DALE, Abraham. (1965).
The Executive Role Constellations. Harvard University, Division of
Research, Graduate School of Business Administration, Boston.

KATZ, E., and EISENSTADT, S. N. (1960). Some Sociological Observations
on the Response of Israeli Organizations to New Immigrants.
Administrative Science Quarterly, 5, 1.

KOMAROVSKY, M. (1946). Cultural Contradictions and Sex Role.
American Journal of Sociology, 50, 184-189.

LEVINSON, D.J. (1959). Role, Personality and Social Structure in the
    Organizational Setting. **Journal of Abnormal and Social Psychology,**
    58, 2, 170-180.
LINTON, R. (1936). **The Study of Man,** New York.
LISSAK, M. and SLUTSKI, N. (ongoing project). Problems of Air-crew
    Training in the Israeli Air Force, mimeo (Hebrew).
MERTON, R.K. (1957). Social Theory and Social Structure, Glencoe,
    The Free Press, especially 9.
NADEL, S.F. (1957). The Theory of Social Structure, Glencoe.
PARSONS, T. (1951). **The Social System,** Glencoe.
REISMANN, L. (1949). A Study of Role Conception in Bureaucracy.
    Social Forces, 27, 305-310.
SARBIN, T.K. (1954). Role Theory, in G. Lindsey (ed.). **Handbook of**
    Social Psychology, Cambridge.
SHILS, E. (1962). The Macrosociological Problem Consensus and
    Dissension in the Larger Society, mimeo.
SOUTHALL, A. (1959). An Operational Theory of Role. **Human Relations,**
    12, 17-34.
TALMON-GARBER, Y. (1955). Differentiation in Collective Settlements.
    Scripta Hierosolymitica, 3.
TALMON-GARBER, Y. (1956). Differentiation in Collective Settlements.
    Scripta Hierosolymitica, 3. Hebrew University, Jerusalem.
TALMON-GARBER, Y. (1959). Structure and Family Size, **Human Relations,**
    12, 2.
THIBAUT, J.W. and KELLY, H.H. (1959). **The Social Psychology of**
    Groups, New York, esp. chs. 8, 9.
TOREN, M. (1965). M.A. Thesis on "Processes of Change in the Role of the
    Bus Driver in Israel" conducted under the supervision of Prof. S.N.
    Eisenstadt (unpublished).
TURNER, R. (1962). Role-Taking, Process Versus Conformity, in Arnold
    M. Rose (ed.). **Human Behavior and Social Processes,** Boston,
    Houghton-Mifflin Com.
WARDEWELL, W. (1952). A Marginal Professional Role: The Chiropractor.
    Social Forces, 30, 339-348.
WEINTRAUB, D. (1964). A Study of New Farmers in Israel. **Sociologia**
    Ruralis, 4, 1.
WEINTRAUB, D. and LISSAK, M. (1961). The Absorption of North African
    Immigrants in Agricultural Settlements in Israel.
    Jewish Journal of Sociology, 3, 1.
WEINTRAUB, D. and LISSAK, M. (1964). Moshav and the Absorption of
    Immigrants, Physical and Material Conditions in the New Moshav,
    and Social Integration and Change. In **Agricultural Planning and**
    Village Community in Israel. J. Ben-David (ed.). Unesco, Paris.

BIOGRAPHICAL NOTES

SHMUEL N. EISENSTADT is Professor of Sociology and Chairman of the Department at the Hebrew University, Jerusalem. He received his Ph. D. from the Hebrew University in 1946.

DOV WEINTRAUB is a Senior Lecturer in Sociology at the Hebrew University, Jerusalem. He received his Ph. D. from this university in 1963.

NINA TOREN is now working for her Ph. D. at Columbia University. She participated in this research while a Research Assistant at the Department of Sociology, the Hebrew University of Jerusalem.